This journal belongs to

....

CHERISHED MOMENTS

Tender Moments to Remember

Baby's First Year Journal
© 2009 Ellie Claire Gift & Paper Corp.
www.ellieclaire.com

Compiled by Joanie Garborg
Designed by Lisa and Jeff Franke for Ellie Claire, Minneapolis, MN

Scripture references are from the following sources: The Holy Bible, New International Version® NIV®. ©
1973, 1978, 1984 by International Bible Society. Used by permission of Zondervan. The NEW AMERICAN
STANDARD BIBLE® (NASB), © Copyright The Lockman Foundation 1960, 1962, 1963, 1968, 1971, 1972,
1973, 1975, 1977, 1995. Used by permission. (www.Lockman.org). The New King James Version (NKJV).
Copyright © 1982 by Thomas Nelson, Inc. Used by permission. The Holy Bible, New Living Translation®
(NLT). Copyright © 1996, 2004. Used by permission of Tyndale House Publishers, Inc., Wheaton, Illinois.
The Message © 1993, 1994, 1995, 1996, 2000, 2001, 2002. Used by permission of NavPress Publishing
Group. The New Century Version® (NCV). Copyright © 1987, 1988, 1991 by Thomas Nelson, Inc. Used by
permission. The Living Bible (TLB) copyright © 1971. Used by permission of Tyndale House Publishers, Inc.,
Carol Stream, Illinois 60188. All rights reserved.

Excluding Scripture verses and poetry, some references to men and masculine pronouns
have been replaced with gender-neutral references.

ISBN 978-1-934770-57-3

Printed in China

tender m*o*ments *to* Remember

Ellie Claire
gift & paper expressions

...inspired by life

Before you were conceived I wanted you; before you were born I loved you; before you were here an hour I would die for you; this is the miracle of love.

MAUREEN HAWKINS

A time for reflection

My dear Little One, I looked forward to your
arrival with anticipation I could barely contain. And
now that you are here, the love I feel for you takes
my breath away. Suddenly my heart is not my own.
Always and forever, it will belong to you.

....

....

....

....

....

....

....

And the Lord loved the baby, and sent congratulations and blessings.

2 SAMUEL 12:24-25 TLB

This is the real gift: we have been given the breath of life, designed with a unique, one-of-a-kind soul that exists forever. Priceless in value, we are hand-crafted by God, who has a personal design and plan for each of us.

WENDY MOORE

....

....

....

....

....

....

....

You wove me in my mother's womb.
I will give thanks to You, for I am fearfully and wonderfully made;
Wonderful are Your works, and my soul knows it very well.

PSALM 139:13-14 NASB

A new baby is like the beginning of all things—
wonder, hope, a dream of possibilities.

EDA J. LESHAN

....

....

....

....

....

....

....

....

....

....

....

....

A poem for Baby

Where did you come from, baby dear?

Out of the everywhere into the here...

How did [it] all just come to be you?

God thought about me, and so I grew.

But how did you come to us, you dear?

God thought about you, and so I am here.

GEORGE MACDONALD

....

....

....

....

....

....

....

*B*y Him all things were created, both in the heavens and on earth, visible and invisible...all things have been created through Him and for Him.

COLOSSIANS 1:16 NASB

A mother's arms are made of tenderness and
children sleep soundly in them.

VICTOR HUGO

A thought for Mommy

In the middle of the night, when all I need
is sleep, you smile and snuggle close and I realize
that sleep wasn't all I needed. When I can hardly
keep my eyes open, you look deep into them and
recognize that I'll always be there for you. I hear you
coo in contentment, and my heart swells to the
melody of the most perfect lullaby of all.

....

....

....

....

....

....

....

I will comfort you as a mother comforts her child.

ISAIAH 66:13 NCV

There is an enduring tenderness in the love of a mother to a [child] that transcends all other affections of the heart.

WASHINGTON IRVING

There is no other closeness in human life like
the closeness between a mother and her baby—
chronologically, physically, and spiritually they are just
a few heartbeats away from being the same person.

SUSAN CHEVER

....

....

....

....

....

....

....

....

*D*on't you see that children are God's best gift?
the fruit of the womb His generous legacy?

PSALM 127:3 THE MESSAGE

*G*od, give me wisdom to see that today is my day with my children;
that there is no unimportant moment in their lives.

HELEN M. YOUNG

....

....

....

....

....

....

....

....

....

....

....

....

....

A prayer from the heart

Your tender smile, your laugh so sweet

Your dear little hands and wiggly feet.

I pray that as your life unfolds

You'll treasure the memories each day holds.

....

....

....

....

....

....

....

....

This is the day the Lord has made; we will rejoice and be glad in it.

PSALM 118:24 NKJV

*A*ngels descending, bring from above
Echoes of mercy, whispers of love.

FANNY J. CROSBY

A lullaby for Baby

Lullaby and goodnight, let angels of light
Spread wings round your bed and guard you from dread.
Slumber gently and deep in the dreamland of sleep,
Slumber gently and deep in the dreamland of sleep.

JOHANNES BRAHMS

....

....

....

....

....

....

....

Don't look down upon a single one of these little children. For I tell you
that in heaven their angels have constant access to My Father.

MATTHEW 18:10 TLB

$\mathscr{A}$ strong sense of family unity, belonging, and warmth doesn't just happen. It is nurtured and grown over time, just as a lovely garden flourishes in the hands of a caring, diligent gardener.

RICHARD PATTERSON JR.

A thought for Mommy

You are the one closest to your baby, the one
who can see the unfolding miracle of uniqueness
wrapped up in your little one. Not every answer for
your one-of-a-kind child can be found in the books.
What you, as a parent, instinctively want to do is
usually the best answer of all.

....

....

....

....

....

....

....

*D*irect your children onto the right path,
and when they are older, they will not leave it.

PROVERBS 22:6 NLT

*he potential possibilities of any child are
the most intriguing and stimulating in all creation.*

RAY L. WILBUR

....

....

....

....

....

....

....

....

....

....

....

....

....

When I approach children, they inspire in me
two sentiments: tenderness for what they are, and
respect for what they may become.

LOUIS PASTEUR

....

....

....

....

....

....

....

....

For the Lord is always good. He is always loving and kind,
and His faithfulness goes on and on to each succeeding generation.

PSALM 100:5 TLB

I wish for you a curiosity that leads you from one wonderful moment to another, and a contentment to be happy wherever you may be.

....

....

....

....

....

....

....

....

....

....

....

....

A wish from the heart

God's bright sunshine overhead,
God's flowers beside your feet...
And by such pleasant pathways led,
May all your life be sweet.

HELEN WAITHMAN

....

....

....

....

....

....

....

....

I will instruct you and teach you in the way which you should go;
I will counsel you with My eye upon you.

PSALM 32:8 NASB

$\mathcal{M}$y precious little child, I pray that you will always know that you are special and loved by the One who created you.

....

....

....

....

....

....

....

....

....

....

....

....

A first song for Baby

Jesus loves me! This I know,
For the Bible tells me so.
Little ones to Him belong;
They are weak, but He is strong.

ANNA B. WARNER

....
....
....
....
....
....
....
....

Jesus said, "Let the little children come to Me, and do not hinder them, for the kingdom of heaven belongs to such as these."

MATTHEW 19:14 NIV

A baby can turn your life upside-down and make it feel right-side up.
A baby can turn your world around and take it in a wonderful new direction.

PHYLLIS HOBE

....

....

....

....

....

....

....

....

....

....

....

....

A thought for Mommy

In the sheltered simplicity of the first days
after a baby is born, one sees again the magical
closed circle, the miraculous sense of two people
existing only for each other.

ANNE MORROW LINDBERGH

....

....

....

....

....

....

....

Turn my way, look kindly on me, as you always do to those
who personally love you.

PSALM 119:132 THE MESSAGE

$\mathcal{M}$ost of all the other beautiful things in life come by twos and threes, by dozens and hundreds. Plenty of roses, stars, sunsets, rainbows, brothers and sisters, aunts and cousins, comrades and friends— but only one mother in the whole world.

KATE DOUGLAS WIGGIN

A time for reflection

What an awesome privilege and joy it is to
know you are irreplaceable in the life of your baby.
Yours is the voice that calms tears, the heartbeat
that comforts, and the kiss that heals. To Baby,
you are a lifeline...the whole world.
There's only one mother!

....

....

....

....

....

....

....

*S*he watches over the affairs of her household....
Her children arise and call her blessed.

PROVERBS 31:27-28 NIV

*T*ell me, what is half so sweet
As a baby's tiny feet.

EDGAR A. GUEST

....

....

....

....

....

....

....

....

....

....

....

....

....

A prayer from the heart

Lord, thank You for this precious child—
The sleepy eyes, the gummy smile,
The wrinkly hands and wiggly feet—
Keep them happy, pure, and sweet.

....

....

....

....

....

....

....

The unfolding of Your words gives light; it gives understanding to the
simple.... Direct my footsteps according to Your word.

PSALM 119:130, 133 NIV

*W*hen the first baby laughed for the first time, the laugh broke into a thousand pieces and they all went skipping about.

SIR JAMES M. BARRIE

....

....

....

....

....

....

....

....

....

....

....

....

....

A poem for Baby

When, for the first time,
I saw your little face—time changed.
It would never again
be counted by the tick of a clock,
but measured instead
by the beat of your heart.

....

....

....

....

....

....

....

Satisfy us in our earliest youth with Your lovingkindness,
giving us constant joy to the end of our lives.

PSALM 90:14 TLB

*Nothing else will ever make you
as happy or as sad,
as proud or as tired,
as motherhood.*

ELLA PARSONS

A thought for Mommy

Be sure to take care of yourself so you can take
care of Baby. As tempting as it is to use nap-time
to catch up on housework, try to sleep when
Baby sleeps. After all, the art of being a parent
is to sleep when the baby isn't looking.

....

....

....

....

....

....

....

....

*B*ut at last the whole earth is at rest and is quiet!
All the world begins to sing!

ISAIAH 14:7 TLB

*M*aking the decision to have a child is momentous. It is to decide forever to have your heart go walking around outside your body.

ELIZABETH STONE

....

....

....

....

....

....

....

....

....

....

....

....

A time for reflection

The very word "motherhood" has an emotional
depth and significance few terms have. It bespeaks
nourishment and safety and sheltering arms.

MARJORIE HOLMES

....

....

....

....

....

....

....

I am with you, and will protect you wherever you go....
I will be with you constantly.

GENESIS 28:15 TLB

A baby is born with a need to be loved—and it never outgrows it.

FRANK A. CLARK

A wish from the heart

I wish you sunshine on your path and
storms to season your journey. I wish you peace—
in the world in which you live and in the smallest
corner of the heart where truth is kept. I wish you
faith—to help define your living and your life.
More I cannot wish you—except perhaps love—
to make all the rest worthwhile.

ROBERT A. WARD

....

....

....

....

....

....

....

....

We have come to know and have believed the love which God has for us.
God is love, and the one who abides in love abides in God.

1 JOHN 4:16 NASB

*F*or the wisdom of the wisest being God has made ends in wonder; and there is nothing on earth so wonderful as the budding soul of a little child.

LUCY LARCOM

A lullaby for Baby

Golden slumbers kiss your eyes,
Smiles awake you when you rise.
Sleep, pretty darling, do not cry,
And I will sing a lullaby.

THOMAS DEKKER

....

....

....

....

....

....

....

The child grew, and the Lord blessed him.

JUDGES 13:24 NKJV

*B*unnies and bears—
Smiles and tears—
Nurseries are where
Love appears.

....

....

....

....

....

....

....

....

....

....

....

....

....

A thought for Mommy

Tiny as they are, babies can already read our
faces and sense our moods. When Baby wakes from a
nap too early, has a too-full diaper at the most
inopportune time, or is inconsolable when you're too
busy, remind yourself that getting things
accomplished isn't nearly as important as
taking time for love.

....

....

....

....

....

....

....

*M*ay the Lord make you increase and abound in love to one another.

1 THESSALONIANS 3:12 NKJV

*E*verything about [the] house had this glow to it.
I think the glow came from Mother.

KATHLEEN COYLE

A time for reflection

When God thought of mother, He must have
laughed with satisfaction, and framed it quickly—
so rich, so deep, so divine, so full of soul, power,
and beauty was the conception!

HENRY WARD BEECHER

....

....

....

....

....

....

....

May the Lord richly bless both you and your children. May you be
blessed by the Lord, who made heaven and earth.

PSALM 115:14-15 NLT

*G*od invented parenthood. He is for us. He is for each of our children. He is champion of their lives, their years, their health, their calling, and their eternal destiny.

RALPH T. MATTSON AND THOM BLACK

A poem for Baby

Now the world is sleeping,

Little stars are peeping,

Father, in thy keeping

May my children rest.

....

....

....

....

....

....

....

....

The Lord will keep you from all harm—He will watch over your life.

PSALM 121:7 NIV

*W*hen you were born, my dear little one, my world screeched to a halt. It ceased to exist. Now it is *our* world.

....
....
....
....
....
....
....
....
....
....
....
....
....

A thought for Mommy

Lifting up that wobbly head, raising up on
pudgy arms—your baby is becoming a regular
wiggle-worm, and the activity level in your home is
about to accelerate. These busy days can be deeply
rewarding with the opportunity to unselfishly give
of your time and pour your love into the life of
your little one.

....

....

....

....

....

....

....

She's up before dawn, preparing breakfast for her family
and organizing her day.

PROVERBS 31:15 THE MESSAGE

To be a child is to know the joy of living.
To have a child is to know the beauty of life.

....

....

....

....

....

....

....

....

....

....

....

....

Because of you
I can be a child once again
I can marvel
at a world full of softness
and see everything
with gentler eyes.

AIDA CANDDINI

....

....

....

....

....

....

....

esus] said, "I tell you the truth, you must change and become like little children. Otherwise, you will never enter the kingdom of heaven."

MATTHEW 18:3 NCV

*G*od's fingers can touch nothing but to mold it into loveliness.

GEORGE MACDONALD

....

....

....

....

....

....

....

....

....

....

....

....

....

Oh God, You have given me a vacant soul,
an untaught conscience, a life of clay. Put Your big
hands around mine.... When my hands mold the clay
of this child's life, may the impressions be, in reality,
made by the movement of Your hands and directed
by Your perfect thoughts.

GLORIA GAITHER

....

....

....

....

....

....

....

O Lord, You are our Father,
We are the clay, and You our potter;
And all of us are the work of Your hand.

ISAIAH 64:8 NASB

*H*old them gentle, hold them sweet—
these little lambs—and guide their feet.

A lullaby for Baby

Sleep, baby, sleep,
Down where the woodbines creep;
Be always like the lamb so mild,
A kind, and sweet, and gentle child.
Sleep, baby, sleep.

MOTHER GOOSE

....

....

....

....

....

....

....

....

He gathers the lambs in His arms and carries them close to His heart.

ISAIAH 40:11 NIV

I've never known such an all-consuming love as I felt the minute this child was born. What absolute joy! What amazing beauty!

....

....

....

....

....

....

....

....

....

....

....

....

It's impossible to spoil your baby with too much
love, too much holding, too much of your presence
and closeness when it's needed. Relax and follow your
heart when your baby cries. Rest assured that
babies are spoil-proof from head to toe.

....

....

....

....

....

....

....

....

*L*ove is patient and kind.... It always trusts, always hopes,
and always endures.

1 CORINTHIANS 13:4, 7 NCV

*H*igher than every painter, higher than every sculptor and than all artists
do I regard the one who is skilled in the art of forming the soul of children.

JOHN CHRYSOSTOM

A time for reflection

I'd rather be a mother than anyone on earth

Bringing up a child or two of unpretentious birth....

I'd rather wash a smudgy face with round,

bright baby eyes—than paint the pageantry of fame,

or walk among the wise.

MEREDITH GRAY

....

....

....

....

....

....

....

*E*very good gift and every perfect gift is from above.

JAMES 1:17 NKJV

I cannot name myself as one who never goes astray,
Who never stumbles on the road, or leaves the hallowed way.
But when I know that baby feet will follow where I've trod,
I walk with care that they too may walk that road that leads to God.

MARGARET FISHBACK POWERS

A prayer from the heart

Help me to give my children good roots, God,
enriched with good music, good talk, good taste; but
above all else, goodness of spirit, goodness of action.

MARJORIE HOLMES

....

....

....

....

....

....

....

*I*n all things show yourself to be an example of good deeds.

TITUS 2:7 NASB

*G*od has blessed us.
He chose us to receive the gift of you.
And I believe with my whole heart
He gave us to you so you might grow in patience, too.

....

....

....

....

....

....

....

....

....

....

....

....

A prayer from the heart

Thank You, Lord, for loving us unconditionally
and for helping us to do the same for our children.
We speak blessings upon all our children, and we
thank You for sending them as blessings to us. Amen.

QUIN SHERRER

....

....

....

....

....

....

....

*Y*ou have chosen to bless my family. Let it continue before You always.
Lord, You have blessed my family, so it will always be blessed.

1 CHRONICLES 17:27 NCV

*S*he is their earth.... She is their food and their bed and
the extra blanket when it grows cold in the night;
she is their warmth and their health and their shelter.

KATHERINE HATHAWAY

....

....

....

....

....

....

....

....

....

....

....

....

....

....

Love me,—I love you,

Love me, my baby...

Mother's arms under you,

Her eyes above you

Sing it high, sing it low,

Love me,—I love you.

CHRISTINA ROSSETTI

....

....

....

....

....

....

....

....

*L*ove one another deeply, from the heart.

1 PETER 1:22 NIV

ortunately for children, the uncertainties of the present always give way to the enchanted possibilities of the future.

CELSEY KIRKLAND

What is the little one thinking about?
Very wonderful things, no doubt;
Unwritten history! Unfathomed mystery!
Yet he laughs and cries, and eats and drinks,
And chuckles and crows, and nods and winks.

JOSIAH GILBERT HOLLAND

....

....

....

....

....

....

....

Our children will live in Your presence.
And their children will remain with You.

PSALM 102:28 NCV

A baby will make love stronger, days shorter, nights longer, bankroll smaller, home happier, clothes shabbier, the past forgotten, and the future worth living for.

....

....

....

....

....

....

....

....

....

....

....

....

A little one brings sunshine into a house and
covers it with a rainbow of promise and hope for the
future. What are your dreams for your baby's future?
How does your child help you to see the whole world
from a new and wonderful point of view?

....

....

....

....

....

....

....

....

*F*or I know the plans I have for you," declares the Lord,
"...plans to give you hope and a future."

JEREMIAH 29:11 NIV

A little face to look at,
A little face to kiss;
Is there anything, I wonder,
That's half so sweet as this?

....

....

....

....

....

....

....

....

....

....

....

....

Heavenly Father, Thank You for the privilege
of having children. Allow every day...to be a
special experience. Help me to savor every moment
that comes, and may my children always be
confident in my love and devotion to them. Amen.

KIM BOYCE

....

....

....

....

....

....

....

God be merciful to us and bless us, and cause His face to shine upon us.

PSALM 67:1 NKJV

May life's greatest gifts always be yours—
happiness, memories, and dreams.

A lullaby for Baby

Sleep, baby, sleep!
Thy father's watching the sheep,
Thy mother's shaking the dreamland tree,
And down drops a little dream for thee.

ELIZABETH PRENTISS

....

....

....

....

....

....

....

*B*e glad for all God is planning for you.
Be patient...and prayerful always.

ROMANS 12:12 TLB

*L*ife is like an exciting book,
and every precious birth starts a new chapter.

Nurture your own soul so that you can nurture
your baby's soul. Go ahead and read the baby books
to educate yourself about your little one's needs and
progress. But also find time to relax, refresh your
spirit, and lose yourself in the pages of a good book.

....

....

....

....

....

....

....

....

*Y*ou watched me as I was...woven together in the dark of the womb.
You saw me before I was born. Every day of my life was recorded in Your book.
Every moment was laid out before a single day had passed.

PSALM 139:15-16 NLT

There was a place in childhood that I remember well,
And there a voice of sweetest tone bright fairy tales did tell,
And gentle word and fond embrace were given with joy to me
When I was in the happy place upon my mother's knee.

SAMUEL LOVER

What is home? A roof to keep out the rain?...
Yes, but home is more than that. It is the laugh of
a baby, the song of a mother, the strength of a father,
warmth of loving hearts, lights from happy eyes,
kindness, loyalty, comradeship...; where even the tea
kettle sings from happiness. That is home.
God bless it!

....

....

....

....

....

....

....

*E*very house has a builder, but the Builder behind them all is God.

HEBREWS 3:4 THE MESSAGE

A young child, a fresh, uncluttered mind, a world before him—to what treasures will you lead him?... There is no greater pleasure than bringing to the uncluttered, supple mind of a child the delight of knowing God and the many rich things He has given us to enjoy.

GLADYS M. HUNT

....

....

....

....

....

....

....

....

....

....

....

Dear Lord, I pray that I will know
the treasures that are hidden in You so I may help
my baby to find the rich things You have given us
to enjoy. Please help me to be an example and
to lead my precious little one into the
delight of knowing You. Amen.

....

....

....

....

....

....

....

Their trust should be in God, who richly gives us all
we need for our enjoyment.

1 TIMOTHY 6:17 NLT

*B*abies are such a nice way to start people.

DON HEROLD

....
....
....
....
....
....
....
....
....
....
....
....
....
....

What are little girls made of?
Sugar and spice and all things nice.
that's what little girls are made of....
What are little boys made of?
Frogs and snails and puppy-dog tails.
that's what little boys are made of.

....

....

....

....

....

....

....

*J*ust as a father has compassion on his children, so the Lord has compassion on those who fear Him. For He Himself knows our frame.

PSALM 103:13-14 NASB

My mother made a brilliant impression upon my childhood life.
She shone for me like the evening star—I loved her dearly.

WINSTON CHURCHILL

....

....

....

....

....

....

....

....

....

....

....

....

A thought for Mommy

Children Learn What They Live

If children live with encouragement,

they learn to appreciate....

If children live with security, they learn to have faith....

If children live with acceptance, and friendship,

they learn to find love in the world.

DOROTHY LAW NOLTE

....

....

....

....

....

....

....

Now, my children, listen to me,
because those who follow my ways are happy.

PROVERBS 8:32 NCV

A child is a quicksilver fountain
spilling over with tomorrows and tomorrows
and that is why she is richer than you or I.

TOM BRADLEY

....

....

....

....

....

....

....

....

....

....

....

....

A time for reflection

Because of you, I love a little more.
Because of you, I take time to give an extra
kiss good-bye.... Because of you, I live today,
before I worry about tomorrow.... Because of you,
I still believe in rainbows. Because of you,
now I can help or listen more.
Because of you, today, I am me.

EILEEN WERNSMAN

....

....

....

....

....

....

....

From His abundance we have all received one
gracious blessing after another.

JOHN 1:16 NLT

Being a full-time mother is one of the highest-salaried jobs in any field since the payment is pure love.

MILDRED B. VERMONT

Mothers are lots of things—doctors, writers,
lawyers, gardeners, actresses, cooks, police officers,
sometimes even truck drivers. And mothers.
Thank You, Lord.

MADELEINE L'ENGLE

....

....

....

....

....

....

....

*G*ive her the reward she has earned,
and let her works bring her praise at the city gate.

PROVERBS 31:31 NIV

*M*ay you have warm words on a cold evening, a full moon on a dark night, and the road downhill all the way to your door.

IRISH BLESSING

....

....

....

....

....

....

....

....

....

....

....

....

A lullaby for Baby

Lullaby and goodnight with lilies of white
And roses of red to pillow your head:
May you wake when the day
Chases darkness away,
May you wake when the day
Chases darkness away.

JOHANNES BRAHMS

....

....

....

....

....

....

....

Those who fear the Lord are secure; He will be a refuge for their children.

PROVERBS 14:26 NLT

$\mathcal{I}$ hope my children look back on today
and see a mom who had time to play.
There will be years for cleaning and cooking,
for children grow up while we're not looking.

I'll show my children right from wrong,
encourage dreams and goals, and through it all
I'll nurture my children's most precious soul!
Though oftentimes a struggle, this job I'll never trade;
for in my hand tomorrow lives...
a future God has made.

....

....

....

....

....

....

....

These commandments that I give you today are to be upon your hearts.
Impress them on your children. Talk about them when you sit at home and
when you walk along the road.

DEUTERONOMY 6:6-7 NIV

*O*f all the joys that lighten suffering on earth,
what joy is welcomed like a newborn child?

C. NEWTON

....

....

....

....

....

....

....

....

....

....

....

....

Children bring freshness and vitality, love and
regeneration to our lives. By loving them, our souls
are healed. God graciously provides relationships
to meet the deep needs of our hearts—primarily a
relationship with Him, but also with those who are
His gifts to us.

....

....

....

....

....

....

....

*H*ow natural it is that I should feel as I do about you,
for you have a very special place in my heart.

PHILIPPIANS 1:7 TLB

*I*t is by tiny steps that we ascend the stars.

JACK LEEDSTROM

....

....

....

....

....

....

....

....

....

....

....

....

A wish from the heart

I wish you love and strength
and faith and wisdom,
Goods, gold enough to help some needy one.
I wish you songs, but also blessed silence,
And God's sweet peace when every day is done.

DOROTHY NELL MCDONALD

....

....

....

....

....

....

....

*I*f you have faith the size of a mustard seed,
you will say to this mountain, "Move from here to there,"
and it will move; and nothing will be impossible to you.

MATTHEW 17:20 NASB

*B*abies come into our earth to bring us fresh blessings from heaven.

A lullaby for Baby

Hush, my dear, lie still and slumber.

Holy angels guard thy bed.

Heavenly blessings without number

Gently falling on thy head.

ISAAC WATTS

....

....

....

....

....

....

....

I will pour out My Spirit on your descendants,
and My blessing on your children.

ISAIAH 44:3 NLT

A mother's love is the deepest of all and
its influences are those that move the world.

They say that man is mighty,
he governs land and sea,
He wields a mighty scepter o'er lesser powers that be;
But a mightier power and stronger
Man from his throne has hurled,
For the hand that rocks the cradle
Is the hand that rules the world.

W. R. WALLACE

....

....

....

....

....

....

....

Children, come and listen to me. I will teach you to worship the Lord.

PSALM 34:11 NCV

*M*otherhood...is the only love I have known that is expansive and that could have stretched to contain with equal passion more than one object.

IRMA KURTZ

Baby dear, God sent you to expand my heart so
that it could contain His great love for you. His love
is limitless, and there was no need to subtract from
somebody else in order to love you more. Every time I
hold you, every time I see your little face, my heart
expands once again.... I'm convinced my enlarged
heart is incurable.

....

....

....

....

....

....

....

*A*nd this I pray, that your love may abound still more and more.

PHILIPPIANS 1:9 NASB

*Children forever hold the whole of their mother's heart in their small hands.
Mothers, in their tender grasp, hold their children's hand for a while
and their heart forever.*

....

....

....

....

....

....

....

....

....

....

....

....

Listen to me, Lord, as a Mother,

and hold me warm, and forgive me.

Soften my experiences into wisdom,

my pride into acceptance,

my longing into trust,

and soften me into love.

T. LODER

....

....

....

....

....

....

....

....

he eternal God is a dwelling place,
and underneath are the everlasting arms.

DEUTERONOMY 33:27 NASB

A babe in the house is a wellspring of pleasure, a resting place for innocence on earth, a link between angels and mankind.

MARTIN FARQUHAR TUPPER

....

....

....

....

....

....

....

....

....

....

....

....

A poem for Baby

Precious baby

you come to me

from where love is infinite

where angels speak a language

only babies understand.

AIDA CANDDINI

....

....

....

....

....

....

....

*H*e has put His angels in charge of you
to watch over you wherever you go.

PSALM 91:11 NCV

The most important thing she'd learned over the years was that there was no way to be a perfect mother and a million ways to be a good one.

JILL CHURCHILL

A thought for Mommy

One of the challenges of motherhood is
that you never know whether you're doing a good job.
But one of the joys is realizing that
when you love your children with all your heart,
mistakes can be forgiven.

....

....

....

....

....

....

....

Most of all, love each other as if your life depended on it.
Love makes up for practically anything.

1 PETER 4:8 THE MESSAGE

Who is queen of baby land?
Mother kind and sweet,
And her love, born above,
Guides the little feet.

....

....

....

....

....

....

....

....

....

....

....

....

A time for reflection

And say to mothers what a holy charge is theirs.
With what a kingly power their love
Might rule the fountains of the newborn mind.

LYDIA H. SIGOURNEY

....

....

....

....

....

....

....

*Y*ou do well when you complete the Royal Rule of the Scriptures:
"Love others as you love yourself."

JAMES 2:8 THE MESSAGE

Just as Jesus took the children, put His hands on them
and blessed them...we can hold our children in our arms,
touching, blessing, and praying over them.

QUIN SHERRER

....

....

....

....

....

....

....

....

....

....

....

....

A prayer from the heart

Heavenly Father, Please help me to develop the
practice of speaking a daily blessing on my children
from the beautifully inspired Scripture, "The Lord
bless you and keep you...." Thank You that even before
little ones can understand the meaning, Your Word
has great power to wonderfully bless and
deeply affect their spirits. Amen.

....

....

....

....

....

....

....

The Lord bless you and keep you; the Lord make His face shine upon you
and be gracious to you; the Lord turn His face toward you and give you peace.

NUMBERS 6:24-26 NIV

*L*ove is the only passion which includes in its
dreams the happiness of someone else.

KARR

....

....

....

....

....

....

....

....

....

....

....

....

....

A lullaby for Baby

Somewhere over the rainbow, way up high
There's a land that I heard of once in a lullaby.
Somewhere over the rainbow skies are blue
And the dreams that you dare to dream
Really do come true.

YIP HARBURG

....

....

....

....

....

....

....

....

Now may the God of hope fill you with all joy and peace in believing,
so that you will abound in hope.

ROMANS 15:13 NASB

*T*he most precious gifts are wrapped in love
and tied up with heartstrings.

....

....

....

....

....

....

....

....

....

....

....

....

....

For all the precious gifts of life

The best must surely be

A baby who brings added joy into a family.

O Little One, so sweet and small,

My wish is that you'll know

The warmth of love and family

Each moment as you grow.

....

....

....

....

....

....

....

*C*hildren are a gift from the Lord; they are a reward from Him.

PSALM 127:3 NLT

$\mathcal{W}$hen you were born, God said, "Yes!"

HENRY WARD BEECHER

A time for reflection

For my dear little child I'd lasso the moon and
give you my love on a silver spoon. I'd run 'round
the world and back again, too, to grant you the hope of
days bright and new. But all that I have and all that I
do is nothing compared to God's love for you.

....

....

....

....

....

....

....

God's love...is ever and always, eternally present to all who fear Him, making
everything right for them and their children as they follow
His Covenant ways.

PSALM 103:17-18 THE MESSAGE

$\mathcal{I}$ remember my mother's prayers, and they have followed me.
They have clung to me all of my life.

ABRAHAM LINCOLN

Heavenly Father, Teach me the importance
of prayer that I may pass that knowledge to my
children. As I tell You my deepest thoughts, fears and
desires in prayer, allow me to hear Your voice speaking
to me in return. May I find Your will for my life as
I learn to listen to You. Amen.

KIM BOYCE

....

....

....

....

....

....

....

All my prayers for you are full of praise to God!
When I pray for you, my heart is full of joy.

PHILIPPIANS 1:3-4 TLB

Tomorrow is tomorrow. Today is bottles, lullabies, and peek-a-boo. Enjoy every minute.

Come to the window, my baby, with me,
And look at the stars that shine on the sea!
There are two little stars that play bo-peep
With two little fish far down in the deep;
And two little frogs cry "Neap, neap, neap";
I see a dear baby that should be asleep.

....

....

....

....

....

....

....

....

Lord, Yours is a household name.
Nursing infants gurgle choruses about You.

PSALM 8:1-2 THE MESSAGE

A lifelong demonstration of lessons learned along the way is the best kind of teaching a child can receive.

....

....

....

....

....

....

....

....

....

....

....

....

A thought for Mommy

I long to put the experience of fifty years at
once into your young lives, to give you at once the
key of that treasure chamber every gem of which has
cost me tears and struggles and prayers, but you must
work for these inward treasures yourself.

HARRIET BEECHER STOWE

....

....

....

....

....

....

....

*P*lace these words on your hearts. Get them deep inside you....
Teach them to your children.

DEUTERONOMY 11:18-19 THE MESSAGE

I actually remember feeling delight at two o'clock in the morning when the baby woke for his feeding, because I so longed to have another look at him.

MARGARET DRABBLE

Your baby is so beautiful! It thrills your
mother-heart with tender gladness just to look at
your tiny and dependent little darling. You would do
anything the baby needs and go to any length to show
your love. How has loving and caring for this baby
enlarged your understanding of God's lavishly
tender heart toward you?

....

....

....

....

....

....

....

How great is the love the Father has lavished on us, that we should be
called children of God! And that is what we are!

1 JOHN 3:1 NIV

Ah! who may read the future? For our darling we crave all blessings sweet
And pray that He who feeds the crying ravens will guide the baby's feet.

ELIZABETH AKERS

....
....
....
....
....
....
....
....
....
....
....
....
....

A wish from the heart

May your little footsteps set you upon a lifetime
journey of love. May you wake each day with His
blessings and sleep each night in His keeping.
And as you grow older, may you always walk in
His tender care.

....

....

....

....

....

....

....

....

*W*alk in the light as He is in the light.

1 JOHN 1:7 NKJV

*E*very material goal, even if it is met, will pass away. But the heritage of children is timeless. Our children are our messages to the future.

BILLY GRAHAM

....
....
....
....
....
....
....
....
....
....
....
....

A poem for Baby

Sleep gently, baby, dream your little dreams,
While I watch your face with love, and wonder
What the future holds in store for you.

K. McLAUGHLAN

....

....

....

....

....

....

....

Lord, You have been our dwelling place in all generations.
Before the mountains were born or You gave birth to the earth and the world,
even from everlasting to everlasting, You are God.

PSALM 90:1-2 NASB

Though motherhood is the most important of all the professions—requiring more knowledge than any other department in human affairs—there was no attention given to preparation for this office.

ELIZABETH CADY STANTON

A thought for Mommy

I have always looked on child rearing not only
as a work of love and duty but as a profession
that was fully as interesting and challenging as any
honorable profession in the world, and one that
demanded the best that I could bring to it.

ROSE KENNEDY

....

....

....

....

....

....

....

*A*s for me and my family, we will serve the Lord.

JOSHUA 24:15 NLT

Two things it is important to give our children—
the first is roots; the other, wings.

....

....

....

....

....

....

....

....

....

....

....

....

....

It will be gone before you know it.
The fingerprints on the wall appear higher
and higher. Then suddenly they disappear.

DOROTHY EVSLIN

....

....

....

....

....

....

....

....

*L*et your roots grow down into Him and draw up nourishment from Him.
See that you go on growing in the Lord.... Let your lives overflow with joy and
thanksgiving for all He has done.

COLOSSIANS 2:7 TLB

God gave us mothers because He knew there are some things only
mothers can do. Stories just she knows that need to be told
that last through the years as memories unfold. God sends us so many
things from above, delivered by mothers and wrapped up in love.

....

....

....

....

....

....

....

....

....

....

....

....

Father, help me to take the time to create
stories with my children. May good memories hold
the generations together. Amen.

SCOTT WALKER

....

....

....

....

....

....

....

*W*e will tell the next generation the praiseworthy deeds of the Lord,
His power, and the wonders He has done...so the next generation
would know them, even the children yet to be born.

PSALM 78:4, 6 NIV

*A*ll mothers are rich when they love their children....
Their love is always the most beautiful of the joys.

MAURICE MAETERLINCK

A poem for Baby

All things bright and beautiful,
All creatures great and small,
All things wise and wonderful,
The Lord God made them all.

CECIL FRANCES ALEXANDER

....

....

....

....

....

....

....

*G*od made everything beautiful in itself and in its time.

ECCLESIASTES 3:11 THE MESSAGE

*W*hat will today hold? Another memory of sharing my life with you.

....

....

....

....

....

....

....

....

....

....

....

....

A thought for Mommy

I meant to do my work today
But a brown bird sang in the apple tree,
And a butterfly flitted across the field,
And all the leaves were calling me.
And the wind went sighing over the land,
Tossing the grasses to and fro,
And a rainbow held out his shining hand—
So what could I do but laugh and go?

RICHARD LEGALLIENNE

....

....

....

....

....

....

....

This is what I have asked of God for you: that you will be encouraged and
knit together by strong ties of love.

COLOSSIANS 2:2 TLB

*E*very child born into the world is a new thought of God,
an ever-fresh and radiant possibility.

KATE DOUGLAS WIGGIN

God sends children for another purpose than
merely to keep up the race—to enlarge our hearts,
to make us unselfish, and full of kindly
sympathies and affections.... My soul blesses
the Great Father every day, that He has
gladdened the earth with little children.

MARY HOWITT

....

....

....

....

....

....

....

The Lord will fulfill His purpose for me;
Your love, O Lord, endures forever.

PSALM 138:8 NIV

*B*abies come wrapped in all our hopes and dreams—but we have to loosen
the wrappings to give them space to grow.

PHYLLIS HOBE

Dear Lord, May my children grow to be
confident...caring for themselves and reaching
out to others. May they have long, successful
lives that grow from failures and errors I have
allowed them to make.... Give me peace and
contentment, and when time marches on,
help me let them go.

MARGARET FISHBACK POWERS

....

....

....

....

....

....

....

*I*t takes wisdom to build a house, and understanding
to set it on a firm foundation.

PROVERBS 24:3 THE MESSAGE

The loveliest masterpiece of the heart of God is the heart of a mother.

THERESE OF LISIEUX

A lullaby for Baby

Lulla, Lulla, sweetly slumber,
Mother's treasure, slumber deep,
Lulla, Lulla, now you're smiling,
Smiling, dear one, through your sleep.

WELSH LULLABY

....

....

....

....

....

....

....

....

These are the children God has given me. God has been good to me.

GENESIS 33:5 NCV

You may have tangible wealth untold;
Caskets of jewels and coffers of gold.
Richer than I you can never be—
I had a mother who read to me.

STRICKLAND GILLILAN

A thought for Mommy

There are benefits in reading together before
Baby can understand what the stories are about. The
more the senses are stimulated, the more development
will occur. Sitting with your little one and reading
aloud is excellent stimulation—and a wonderful
shared activity that you can enjoy together for
years to come.

....

....

....

....

....

....

....

*Y*ou took in the sacred Scriptures with your mother's milk!
There's nothing like the written Word of God for showing you the way
to salvation through faith in Christ Jesus.

2 TIMOTHY 3:15-16 THE MESSAGE

A child's hand in yours—what tenderness and power it arouses.
You are instantly the very touchstone of wisdom and strength.

MARJORIE HOLMES

One of the greatest experiences in life is to have
a child fall asleep...in your arms. There are things in
life that are memorable, even exhilarating—climbing
the Rockies, laughing past midnight with friends,
hitting a home run. But a trusting child asleep
in your arms is the ultimate.

WILLIAM L. COLEMAN

....

....

....

....

....

....

....

Whoever welcomes a little child like this in My name welcomes Me.

MATTHEW 18:5 NIV

No one can fully measure the blessings that come to the life
of the one who has a praying mother.

ROY LESSIN

A prayer from the heart

Father in Heaven, I feel such responsibility for
this indescribably precious and complex little person
You have placed in my life. Thank You that You will
give me the grace and wisdom I need to guide my baby
in Your ways. I'm so grateful that You hear
and answer my prayers. Amen.

....

....

....

....

....

....

....

Their children will be successful everywhere;
an entire generation of godly people will be blessed.

PSALM 112:2 NLT

The birds upon the tree-tops sing their song,
The angels chant the chorus all day long,
The flowers in the garden blend their hue,
So why shouldn't I, why shouldn't you
Praise Him too?

....

....

....

....

....

....

....

....

....

....

....

A poem for Baby

Darling baby, infant fair,
nature's gift, my answered prayer;
birdies sing for you and me
such a tender melody.

AIDA CANDDINI

....

....

....

....

....

....

....

....

I prayed for this child, and the Lord answered my prayer
and gave him to me.

1 SAMUEL 1:27 NCV

One of the best things a parent can do for a child is make the child feel that
home is the safest and happiest place in the world.

A thought for Mommy

I once asked one of my smaller children what
he thought a home was and he replied, "It's a place
where you come in out of the rain." The home
should be a warm sanctuary from the storms of life....
A haven of love and acceptance. Not only children,
but [parents] need this security.

GIGI GRAHAM TCHIVIDJIAN

....

....

....

....

....

....

....

He blesses the home of the righteous.

PROVERBS 3:33 NIV

Loving a child is a circular business...the more you give, the more you get; the more you get, the more you want to give.

PENELOPE LEACH

A mother's love is like a circle, it has no
beginning and no ending. It keeps going around
and around...touching everyone who comes in contact
with it. Engulfing them like the morning's mist,
warming them like the noontime sun, and covering
them like a blanket of evening stars.

ART URBAN

....

....

....

....

....

....

....

*L*et Your unfailing love surround us, Lord, for our hope is in You alone.

PSALM 33:22 NLT

$\mathcal{C}$hildren of the heavenly Father safely in His bosom gather;
Nestling bird nor star in heaven such a refuge e'er was given.

CAROLINA BERG